The Blame Game

Julie Chapus

The Blame Game
Author: Julie Chapus

Copyright ©2013, 2014 Julie Chapus.
Christforkidsministries.com
ISBN 978-1-935018-87-2
All rights reserved by author

PUBLISHED BY:
Five Stones Publishing
A DIVISION OF:
The International Localization Network
randy2905@gmail.com
ILNcenter.com

Most of the scripture cited in this book has been paraphrased by the author. Chapter and verse references are provided throughout the text.

Scriptures taken from the Zondervan Life Application Study Bible, New International Version © 1988,1989,1990,1991 by Tyndale House Publishers, Inc., Wheaton, IL, 60189

Inspired by God
Written by Julie Chapus © 2013, 2014

Thank You

Thank you so much Heavenly Father. I am humbled over what you have done and continue to do in my life. Although I am nothing but dust and ashes you have given me life, and one that is beyond my wildest imagination. I love you Father and can't wait to see what you will do next.

Dedication

This book is dedicated to you, Dave. And you thought all these years that I didn't care about sports! I love you.

Special Thanks

I am so grateful to the editors of this book, David Chapus and Jennifer Edwards, for your continued support.

Special thanks to my mentor, Rev. B.R. VanDame Weirich; your prayers and suggestions have made this book everything the Lord wants it to be.

Thanks to my parents who have continued to support me in all my endeavors.

Thank you so much 5 Stones Publishing. May this book help many children and their families.

Thank you Pastor Josh and everyone at Elim Gospel Church for your encouragement and support.

To Mandy: Your prayers and encouragement have helped me to persevere and never give up. Thank you!

Contents

The Blame Game

Blame exists in our world; it is all around us. Take your mom or dad, for example—have they ever blamed you when something bad happened around the house?

Let's say you're playing with something that belongs to your parents, and you accidentally break it. When your parents ask you about it, do you ever think about blaming someone else, like your brother or sister or the cat? It's OK, we've all been caught red-handed. That means we have all been caught doing things we knew we shouldn't have been doing. When that happens, it's tempting to try to shift the blame to someone or something else.

When we do that, it just keeps the "blame game" going. What I mean is that once we blame someone for one thing, it gets easier and easier to blame people and situations for other things, until we find ourselves blaming again and again for just about everything bad in our lives.

When we fall into this pattern, it actually hurts us, because we get stuck in a cycle that goes nowhere. It's kind of like walking in a circle that never ends and never gets us to where we want to go. It just keeps taking us right back to blame. At some point our goal should be to stop that cycle and get blame out of our lives. It will help us feel better inside, and it will help the people around us too.

God is not a fan of the blame game. He knows in this game we all get hurt and He also knows that blame keeps us from the awesome path He has prepared for us. God's path always leads us to peace and love.

God loves us so much that He has given us many teachings about blame and why it does not belong in our lives. He's done that so we can live out a much more fulfilled life. God helps us this way because He wants us to have peace and love in our hearts, and He wants us to feel joy; not hate, blame, fear or emptiness.

As we move through this first chapter we will explore why blame exists and where it may occur in our lives. Later on, we'll look at some ways to deal with blame and how to avoid falling into the blame game.

* * * * * *

So why is there so much blame in our world, and where does it come from? Let's turn to God's word to find out.

When God first created our world, everything was very different from the way it is today. Everything was perfect.

You see, God is love, and when He made the Universe, our world knew nothing but love. There was nothing bad; "bad" didn't even exist. There was no such thing as hate, blame, illness, or disease. That's why the Bible tells us in Genesis 1:31 that "God saw all that He had made, and it was very good."

The world was so beautiful, in fact, it's hard to imagine what it must have been like, because things are so different now. It's difficult for us to think of a perfect world, because the world we live in has many problems; it is definitely not perfect.

So what happened? How did the world go from being good in all ways to being imperfect, with so many problems? That's a good question, and if we turn to our Bible, we will find the answers.

After He made the earth, God created a man named Adam and a woman named Eve. The Bible tells us in Genesis 1:27, "So God created man in his own image, in the image of God he created him; male and female he created them." God—who is perfect and loving—made Adam and Eve out of His perfect love.

When Adam and Eve were created, they were living with God in a place called the Garden of Eden. God specifically told Adam and Eve they were not to eat the fruit from a certain tree in the garden, called the tree of knowledge. We'll see why it was called that in a moment, but for now, the important thing is that God knew the fruit of this tree would be very bad for Adam and Eve. That's why He warned them to stay away from that tree, and not to eat it's fruit. (See Genesis 2:16-17)

But Adam and Eve didn't listen to God. They did eat fruit from the forbidden tree. And immediately, bad things started to happen.

We are told in the Bible (Genesis 3:8-10), "Then the man and his wife heard the sound of the Lord God as he was walking in the garden in the cool of the day, and they hid from the Lord God among the trees of the garden. But the Lord God called to the man, 'Where are you?' Adam answered, 'I heard you in the garden and I was afraid because I was naked, so I hid.'"

I know this can be hard to understand, but when Adam and Eve were living in the Garden of Eden with God, they had nothing to hide, or to hide from. There was no embarrassment or shame. Remember, up until this point everything was perfect. "Wrong" didn't even exist. We cannot understand this fully, because we do live in a world where bad things happen every day, but up until this point, Adam and Eve knew nothing but goodness and love.

But once they ate that fruit from the tree of knowledge, Adam and Eve became aware of good and evil. That is when sin came into their lives. Sin is a violation of God's law, which is also sometimes called divine law. ("Divine" means that it comes from God.) The divine law for Adam and Eve was, "Don't eat that fruit." But Adam and Eve broke God's rule.

In that moment they became full of fear. We see Adam and Eve feeling afraid for the first time. We see them hiding from God, and soon we will see blame enter the picture too.

That's why the tree was called the tree of knowledge of good and evil—after they ate its fruit, Adam and Eve knew the difference between right and wrong, and between good and evil. And they knew that they had done something wrong by disobeying God.

So when Adam told God that he hid because he was naked, God asked, "Who told you that you were naked? Have you eaten from the tree that I commanded you not to eat from?" (Genesis 3:11)

Now watch how Adam responded to God. Adam said, "The woman you put here with me—

she gave me some fruit from the tree, and so I ate it." (Genesis 3:12)

Do you see what Adam did there? First he blamed God for giving him the woman, and then he blamed the woman for giving him the fruit.

Next, God turned to Eve and asked, "What is this you have done?" (Genesis 3:13) The woman answered God by blaming a serpent that was in the garden. Eve said, "The serpent deceived me so I ate." (Genesis 3:13) So Adam blamed God and Eve, and Eve blamed the serpent.

I'm sure Adam and Eve were very frightened at this point. They had never disobeyed God before, and the first time they did, they went from feeling perfect love to being terrified and wanting to hide from God. Not only that, they both started blaming others for what they had done.

This all happened so fast. Suddenly the life Adam and Eve had known changed radically. They felt different inside, and their whole world changed too. From that time on, sin entered the world, and along with it came all the bad emotions that sin brings, like fear, doubt, and blame.

After this happened, Adam and Eve were no longer able to live in the Garden of Eden, because only perfect love could exist there. Adam and Eve were now exposed to both good and evil, and they knew it. This meant they would have to make choices now: choices to either live in a good way or in a way that would lead to sin.

From that point on, life became very difficult for them, and the problems that Adam and Eve had to face are still with us today. We are all affected by the knowledge of good and evil. Every day we must make choices. Sometimes we make good choices, and other times the choices we make lead us into sin. We all have to make these choices based on our free will. That means we have the freedom to choose things that lead us into sin, or things that lead us to love and peace.

God always wants to help us make the right choices, but He never forces us to do anything. He loves us so much that He leaves the decisions up to us. But when we choose to follow God, we gain an incredible sense of peace and love in our hearts. When we choose to follow things that lead us to sin, we get overwhelmed with bad feelings that take our peace away, and we always get hurt.

* * * * * * *

Like Adam and Eve, we all know what it is like to be afraid. We have all felt like hiding when we've done something wrong, we have all lied, and if we are honest with ourselves, I am sure that we can think of times in our lives when we too have blamed someone else for something we've done. These things all have to do with sin.

Well, thank God for our Bible. In it, God gives us wisdom we can use, and illustrations that we can learn from and apply to our daily lives. God even sent His Son Jesus to the earth to help us overcome all the problems of sin, by teaching us how God wants us to live. God has also provided us with many ways to respond to any bad situation we may find ourselves in, including those times when we are tempted to blame others.

In the Gospel of Luke, Jesus teaches us some things about blame. One day someone told Jesus about some people from a place called Galilee, who had gone through some terrible suffering. Jesus replied, "Do you think that those Galileans were worse sinners than all the other Galileans because they suffered this way? I tell you no!" (Luke 13:2) What Jesus meant was that just because something bad happens to someone does not mean that it must be their fault or that they must be bad people.

You see, we all sin. That means we all do things at times that we know we should not do. And that is why it's not right for us to look at someone else and blame them for their problems. This is also sometimes known as judging others.

God knows we tend to do this, and Jesus wants to help us stop judging and blaming others, because He knows these behaviors hurt all of us. In Luke 6:37, Jesus says, "Do not judge and you will not be judged. Do not condemn and you will not be condemned. Forgive and you will be forgiven. Give and it will be given to you. A good measure pressed down, shaken together and running over will be poured into your lap. For with the measure you use, it will be measured to you."

None of us wants to be judged or blamed, so we should not do this to others. We want to be forgiven when we mess up, so we should forgive others too. In short, we should treat others the way we would like to be treated. That's known as the Golden Rule, and it's another of Jesus' teachings. We can find it in Luke 6:31: "Do to others as you would have them do to you."

I love this teaching. When I think about how I would want to be treated, it really does help me to treat other people better.

All we need to do is think of the times we have been in trouble; would we want someone to help us, or would we want someone to blame us for our problems? I'm sure most of us would want help, and that is why we should treat others in a helpful way too. If we find that we are blaming others more than helping them, the following prayer may help.

Prayer

Dear Jesus, please help me treat other people the way I would want to be treated, please give me compassion in my heart for others, and teach me to pray for those who are hurting.

Amen.

What Jesus really wants is for all of us to show love and compassion for each other. In the Gospel of John (John 13:34), Jesus states, "A new command I give you: love one another. As I have loved you, so you must love one another. By this everyone will know that you are my disciples [followers], if you love one another." What a great rule to live by!

During His time on earth, Jesus spread this message of love, and He taught us how to love each other. When we pray for others, that is loving them. When we see bad things happening to other people, we should always pray for them. When people make us angry, we should pray for them too.

God does not want us to go around blaming and being mean to each other. He knows that when we do that, we hurt ourselves and others. But even though our world has sin and bad things in it, if we follow God's ways and love one another, we can have peace and love in our hearts. Not only that, we will be able to help others have peace and love as well. Now that sounds really awesome!

It would be wise, then, for us to take a look at how Jesus wants us to live. The things He taught us will bring peace and love to our lives, if we are willing to follow them. That means not just reading about Jesus' teachings, but actually making them a part of our daily lives.

* * * * * * *

One important thing to keep in mind is that we may be tempted to play the blame game not just when we've done something wrong (as in our example earlier of breaking something that belongs to your parents), but when someone else has been mean to us. If something gets said that hurts our feelings, or if someone treats us badly, we may get angry at them, blame them for being mean to us, and want to get even by hurting them too. Or we might even blame ourselves, thinking that we must have done something to deserve to be treated that way. None of this does us or anybody else any good. It will only cause more hurt and bad feelings.

The only way we will be able to get out of these bad habits is to turn to God and follow His ways. Again, let's look at what Jesus has to say to us about this. In Matthew 5:44, Jesus says, "Love your enemies, and pray for those who persecute (harm) you."

Now remember, we can have peace if we do what Jesus asks us to do. If we truly are angry at someone right now and blaming them for hurting us, let's use this teaching as our very first tool, and pray for that person, even if they have hurt us badly.

You might wonder, why should we pray for those who hurt us? Well, Jesus, who is God's Son, knows this is going to be good for us. When we forgive those who have hurt us, and pray for them, we actually feel much better inside than when we carry our hurt and anger inside.

Jesus also knows that when we pray for someone who's hurt us, we can help that person too. And that's important, because that person is probably hurting on the inside as well.

When a person hurts someone, it's usually because they themselves have been hurt, and are struggling with a lot of bad feelings. But if we are willing to do things God's way, He can heal our pain, and He can help the person who hurt us. That is great news, because it means all of us can have love and peace in our lives, and stop hurting others.

We may have to keep a safe distance from the people who hurt us, but let's not allow that to stop us from praying for these people.

If there is someone in your life that has hurt you, the following prayer may help.

Prayer

Dear Jesus, I have been blaming (name the person) for the hurt I have suffered. I know I have done things wrong in the past. Please forgive me for my wrongdoing and help me forgive (name person). Please bless (name person) and heal (his/her) heart, and please heal my heart too. Help us all to stop hurting.

Thank you, Jesus.

Amen.

Can you see how prayer spreads love? There is a lot of blame in our world, and so much anger. When we lash out at people, it only spreads more anger and blame, and we certainly don't need any more of that in our lives.

But when we make an effort to stop blaming others, and to pray for them instead, we spread God's love. And that's good for all of us. Here's another prayer that you may find helpful.

Prayer

Dear God, please forgive me for blaming others for my hurt. Please bless the people I have been blaming and heal them from any hurt I may have caused them. I also ask that you please heal me too, and help me to stop blaming.

Amen.

* * * * * * *

Another reason why we blame or judge others is that it can give us a false feeling of being better or more important than others. We may think we are superior to them. That is not God's way, though, so it does not work. It is a lie. If we believe this lie that we are more important than somebody else, it will actually end up causing us more pain, because we will lose our feelings of peace and love inside.

The truth is that God loves each of us the same. In the Bible (Romans 2:11) we are told, "God does not show favoritism." It's true. In God's eyes, we are all equal because we are all His children! He made each one of us and He loves us all the same, so trying to put other people down and blaming them for our bad feelings is never going to lead us to a life of peace and happiness. It will certainly never make us more important than anyone else in God's eyes. We are actually going against God when we do these kinds of things.

The funny thing about all of this is that we really *are* important to God; we don't need to put other people down to try to make ourselves seem or feel important. God made us and He loves us. He has a great plan for our lives. Jeremiah 29:11 states, "For I know the plans I have for you, declares the Lord. Plans to prosper you and not to harm you, plans to give you hope and a future."

Let's think about that for a moment. God our Father, our Creator who loves us, has a plan for each and every one of us. He wants to give us hope and a future. How amazing is that!

It makes me wonder, though, why don't we always seem to believe it? Maybe some of us just don't realize this truth, or maybe it's because we have been blaming God for our problems. I know it's hard to face up to, but sometimes we really do blame God for our struggles. It's OK to admit it if you have done this; lots of us have.

As I was praying on this, God led me to some passages in the Bible. The first passage is Proverbs 19:3, which states, "A man's own folly ruins his life, yet his heart rages against the Lord."

What this proverb is telling us is that sometimes we make bad choices or decisions, and as a result we can get into trouble and start having problems. When that happens, we may be apt to blame God for our problems. Instead of being willing to admit that our troubles might have been caused by our own actions, we get angry at God.

Remember, this has been happening ever since Adam and Eve. Adam blamed God for creating the woman, saying that she had given him the fruit to eat, but Adam knew he was not supposed to eat the fruit. It was not God's fault what happened; Adam and Eve did something wrong. They chose to eat the fruit. They disobeyed God's instructions, and that's what led to their problems.

Sometimes we need to admit that we make bad choices, and that we sin. It's OK, because God is our helper. He is not the cause of our problems. The Bible tells us in Lamentations 3:33, "He does not willingly bring affliction or grief to the children of men." And Psalm 46:1 says, "God is our refuge and strength, an ever-present help in trouble."

That's why Jesus came to the earth. God knew we needed His help to overcome blame and sin in our lives. That's why He has given us instructions, so that we can avoid these pitfalls. But if we do fall into sin—and we all do—God is our help out of it.

Because God loves us, He wants to help us overcome our problems. If we can learn to turn to Him instead of blaming Him, He will give us clear instructions on how to get out of the messes we may find ourselves in.

God is not our enemy, He is our only help. If we are angry at God over something, we should tell Him why we are angry. We should share with Him everything that is in our hearts and minds. It's good for us to give even the worst thoughts and feelings we have to God. He can handle it. He wants to help us, but we must be honest with Him about our thoughts and feelings. He will help us through this, but it starts with honesty and prayer.

Prayer

Dear God, I am angry and I have been blaming you. (Tell God what it is you have been blaming him for.) Please help me out of this mess I am in. Please forgive me for blaming You, too. I need You, Lord. I know Your ways are good and You are my helper. Please help me to remove this blame and anger from my life, and please clean my heart. Thank You, Lord Jesus.

Amen.

Once we admit our wrongdoing to God and turn to Him, a sense of peace and love will enter our hearts. That's when we will know and understand, and truly believe the message that God really does love us. Learning God's ways becomes exciting to us. Living according to His ways will make us feel wonderful, alive, and full of energy. Knowing God loves us will fill us with so much peace, we won't want to hold on to any feelings that take that peace away. So let's focus on God and His plan for our lives, rather than spending one more minute holding onto hate, anger and blame.

* * * * * * *

As I was praying about other ways that we may fall into blame, something else came to me that I would like to share with you.

We all want to know that someone cares about us and loves us. And that's where a lot of us go wrong.

Here's what I mean. We sometimes look to other people to fill us with the love that only God can give us. We all want and need God's love, but when we go to someone else for that love, it can cause us and them a lot of problems and pain. How? Sooner or later we're bound to discover that other people have just as many weaknesses as we do, and they're just as imperfect as we are. When that happens, it can lead us to blame them for not being able to give us what we need, and that can cause us to feel angry at them and treat them badly.

Lots of people fall into this pattern of making friends, and getting into relationships, thinking, "If I can make them happy, then they will love me, and everything will be all right." This can lead to a destructive cycle and a false sense of love, because no person can make us happy and give us all the love we need all the time. Only God can do that. We will end up being let down, and so will the people around us, whenever we put our relationships with them before our relationship with God.

Now there's nothing wrong with having friends, or making people happy. Jesus himself had friends here on earth, and we can certainly have friends too. And we should love other people. Jesus even instructs us to love one another. But He also told us there is something very important we should do first.

Jesus said, "Love God with all your heart, and with all your soul, and with all your strength, and with all your mind, and love your neighbor as yourself." (Luke 10:27) So first, we are to love God and be filled with His love. Then, and only then, will we be able to love others in a healthy and godly way. We can try to love other people without God's love, but sooner or later we will find ourselves playing the blame game.

If we find that we care more about pleasing other people than following God's ways, or if we think that other people's love is the most important thing in our lives, we will eventually hurt ourselves and them. If we are stuck in this pattern right now, the first thing we should do is turn to God, because He can stop this cycle. Here's a prayer to help us do that.

Prayer

Dear God, please forgive me for putting other people in Your place. Your love is really what I need, Lord. Please fill me with Your love so that I may love others in Your way. Help me turn to You with all my heart, God.

Amen.

* * * * * * *

So far, we have discovered the reasons why blame exists in our world and in our lives. We have also seen some different reasons why we may blame others, and how that affects us. So what more is there to learn?

The next several chapters of this book will explore Jesus' teachings to help us overcome the kinds of problems we've been talking about. We will also look at ways we can guard against blame and sin in our lives by looking at real-life examples. As we move forward in the following chapters, please keep these words of Jesus in your mind and in your heart. They will help you, and they will also give you the strength to face anything you may be going through.

You may find it helpful to say this next verse out loud.

Jesus' Words of Encouragement

John 16:33 ~ I have told you these things so that in me you may have peace. In this world you will have trouble. But take heart! I have overcome the world.

Key Players

Remember how in Jeremiah 29:11, God said He has a plan for us? Well, God knows that His plans are good for us and for all the people around us. God also knows that if we seek to live out His plan for our lives, we will have peace and feel satisfied inside, because we will be doing what God created us to do.

Ephesians 2:10 tells us, "We are God's workmanship created in Christ Jesus to do good works, which God prepared in advance for us to do."

This is great news! God has such wonderful things in store for us. He wants what's best for us, but we cannot get there if we carry hate, blame, and anger around inside us. Holding onto these feelings is only going to hurt us and others, and remember, God's ultimate goal is to bring us back to a place of peace and love.

That is why Jesus came to help us. He knows we can have peace and love, but in order to do that we need to follow Him. We can start by being honest with ourselves and with God about the thoughts and feelings we hold onto. Jesus Himself has told us, "If you hold to my teaching you are really my disciples. Then you will know the truth and the truth will set you free." (John 8:31-32)

Getting honest about our attitudes and thoughts can help us get our lives back on track, and to walk with God. Walking with God has to do with how we live our daily lives: what kinds of things we think about, and the attitudes we hold about ourselves and others. When we walk with God, we have a deep feeling of peace.

When we are on the wrong path though, we may feel anxious, fearful, and worried. Those feelings are an indication that our thoughts may not be the kind of thoughts that will lead us to carry out God's good plan for our lives. Our attitudes about ourselves and others may need some adjustments as well.

The best thing we can do is turn to God and let Him know what sort of thoughts and feelings we have been having. We may find, for example, that we have been having angry thoughts all day, or we may realize that our thoughts have been focused on what other people have said and done to us.

When we realize that our thoughts are not lining up with the teachings of Jesus, we shouldn't feel discouraged, because this awareness is a powerful tool for us. It will help us get back on the path to following God's ways.

If you know that some of your thoughts and feelings are not what God would want you thinking or feeling, the first thing to do is pray. Let's ask God now to show us the truth about our thoughts and attitudes so we can change them and allow God to get us back to feelings and thoughts of peace and love.

Prayer

Dear God, Please help me change whatever in my life is not pleasing to You. Forgive me and help me to see the truth about my attitudes and thoughts, so that You may truly set me free. Help me to think your thoughts and to change my attitudes, so that I may have peace, not only for myself but for all the people around me.

Amen.

Next, we should ask God to help us become a *key player*. On a team, a key player is a player that the rest of the team, from the coach on down, knows they can count on. When the game is on the line, a key player is the player everyone else will look to, to make the big play.

But being a key player isn't limited to sports. In life, a key player is someone who tells the truth and follows through, even when that isn't easy to do. Key players do what they say they will do, and they do it with a good attitude.

Jesus said, "Simply let your yes be yes and your no be no." (Matthew 5:37) What did Jesus mean by that? In part, it has to do with our character; in other words, the kind of person we are.

Imagine you ask two friends—let's call them Danny and Sarah—to meet you at a certain place and time. Danny says, "I promise I'll be there, on time, cross my heart. You can count on me." Sarah simply says, "Yes, I'll be there."

But when the time comes, only Sarah is there. Danny never shows up. Later he tells you that he forgot.

Who acted better in that situation, Danny or Sarah? Sarah, of course. Why? Because she followed through on what she said she would do. This is also called being reliable.

And Danny? Well, his words were much stronger than Sarah's; he promised he'd be there. But since he didn't keep his promise, that doesn't mean much, does it?

When we don't follow through with what we say we will do, that can make us feel bad about ourselves, and it can make other people feel bad too, especially when they were depending on us. That's why Jesus wants our yes to be yes, and our no to be no. All the promises in the world won't do anybody any good if we don't keep them. Better just to say a simple "yes" or "no" and then follow through than to make big promises that we can't or won't keep.

When we consistently stick to what we say we will do, we build something called integrity. The words we say will hold weight. People will know that when we say "yes," we mean it, and they will be able to rely on us. They'll know we are key players.

Jesus is a great example. He is the best key player there is. His word is truth and we can trust Him. He means what He says and He says what He means. When we follow His ways, Jesus opens doors for us and He helps us become the key players He created us to be.

But what if we haven't been a key player before now? Can we really change things around in our lives? With God's help, yes we can. Even if we have not kept our word in the past, even if we have made promises and broken them, God can help us change everything right now. It may take time for other people to change their opinions about us, especially if we have let them down repeatedly. We may also need to gain confidence in ourselves, because we know that we haven't always been reliable in the past.

We are not stuck though; in fact with God's help, we can change things right now! And as other people begin to notice how much better we are acting, thinking, and feeling, they just might want to ask Jesus for help in their own lives too.

If we know our character is not what God wants it to be, if our yes does not mean yes, and if our no does not mean no, then the following prayer may be of help.

Prayer

Dear God, please help me have better character. I want to obey You and do things Your way. I am going to need help with this, because right now I am not very dependable, but I know You can help me fix this. Help me be the Key Player you made me to be. Thank You, Father.

Amen.

If you find this difficult to do, remember Jesus's Words of Encouragement.

John 16:33 ~ I have told you these things so that in me you may have peace. In this world you will have trouble. But take heart! I have overcome the world.

The Game Changer

As I was working on this book, my husband brought home a video called *Undefeated*. This documentary movie was about a real-life high school football coach named Bill Courtney. He cared about his team and his players so much that he helped each player individually build character, using football as a tool. He did this by putting Jesus' teachings into practice in the game, and he taught his players how to apply those same lessons in their everyday lives.

One of the most important messages coach Courtney shared was that a person's character is not revealed in victory, but in defeat. Coach Courtney said, "Our true character shows itself most clearly when the chips are down—when we are losing and when things are not going well; that's when we reveal what kind of people we really are."

It's easy to be nice, and kind, and cheerful, when everything is going great. As coach Courtney taught his players, anyone can handle being a champion, but not everyone can lose with their character intact. When we are winning and things are good, of course we feel good about ourselves.

Everything seems wonderful, and it's easy to be happy and have a great attitude during those times.

But when we are losing and things aren't so good, whether in a game or in our lives, it's not so easy to maintain our good character. We may not treat ourselves or others the way we ought to. Even worse, we may start blaming others for our losing attitudes.

At one point in the video, coach Courtney's football team had lost a bunch of games. A lot of the players also had personal problems to deal with. Some had injuries, others had troubles at home involving their families. We saw many of the players struggling with a lot of emotional pain, and that was causing them to make poor decisions. Some of them were fighting with their teammates too. It's so difficult to act and think well, when all we are focused on is the bad things in our lives. And when bad things are happening, it's all too easy to focus on those bad things, to the point where we hardly seem able to think about anything else.

During these times, coach Courtney often prayed with his players. He always reminded them to keep a good character by following Jesus' teachings. They did that by always doing the right thing, no matter what, and by treating others well, no matter how others were treating them. The coach taught his players to stop blaming others for their problems, and he encouraged them to keep their eyes on God.

We also saw how difficult this was for some of them to do, especially when they had so many problems to deal with. But coach Courtney just kept reminding his players how good God is. We saw the players start to focus on the good things coach was saying to them, instead of on their problems. And we watched God bless these players. We saw God do awesome things in these guys' lives. It was amazing to watch God transform these young men into great players with great character.

Coach Courtney made a big impact on these players' lives, but all he really did was speak God's words to his players and teach them Jesus's ways. It does not seem like much, but that was the game changer for everyone. When the guys were able to focus on the good in their lives and put these teachings into practice, both on the field and off, they were able to overcome their problems, make better decisions and treat each other much better.

This was so encouraging because it showed clearly that God's ways work, and that any one of us can follow them. It's just so fantastic to see God work in our lives when we turn to Him. God's ways are for all of us. As long as we turn to Him we can live a life full of victory too.

As we study Jesus' character, we discover some very interesting things about Him. Did you know, when people were mean to Jesus and when they blamed Him for things, He never made threats back at them. Instead, He prayed for them. He never hurt anyone or tried to get revenge. Instead He prayed that God would forgive the people who had hurt Him. Even when people were putting Jesus to death, He prayed, "Father, forgive them, for they do not know what they are doing." (Luke 23:34)

How many times have we done things in our lives or made choices that hurt ourselves or others without even realizing it? This is an important question. I can remember times in my life when I did not do anything God's way. I was always full of fear and I was struggling with a lot of bad emotions. I would feel anxious and be afraid of not doing everything perfectly. This caused me so much stress that I became very short-tempered. I would snap at people and say mean things without even realizing how badly I was treating others. I knew I was stressed out but I didn't realize how that stress was making me react to people. I was so focused on how bad I felt I didn't realize how poorly I was treating those around me.

At that time, then, I had a lot of bad character traits. (I will share more of them in the section of this book titled "I Quit!") But when I started to live by Jesus' teachings and actually put them into practice, I was amazed at how much better my life got.

Now I don't want to leave you with a false impression that once we start to follow God, all of our problems are going to magically disappear. When we read the Bible, it is clear that problems are simply a part of life for everyone.

So yes, we all have problems, but when we turn to God, something very special happens to us. There is a peace that enters our hearts. That's exactly what happened to me. The fear I used to feel was no longer in control of me. The anxiety and worry seemed to just vanish. The more I started to learn about Jesus, and the more I started following His teachings in the Bible, the more peace I started to feel.

The more peace I felt, the more peaceful my behavior became, and I started treating others better. I hadn't even been aware how mean I had been to people at times until I received this peace. I was certainly not problem-free, but I knew in my heart and my mind that I was OK, because God truly loved me, and I knew He was with me. And that helped me to become calmer and much more caring about those around me.

I really wanted to share this with you, because just as God helped that football team in *Undefeated*, and just as He has helped me, He can help you too. Jesus is for everybody; He can help all of us. He really knows what He is talking about. He is God's Son, and we are all wise to learn from His teachings, and apply them to our lives.

If you are struggling with negative emotions right now that are hurting you, they may be hurting others too. The following prayer may help.

Prayer

Dear God, I have been struggling with (explain your problem). I can see that this is hurting me and it may be hurting those around me too. Please forgive me, Lord, and please heal anyone I may have hurt. I pray that You will help me overcome this problem in my life. Help me to learn and live Your ways.

Amen.

Let's never forget Jesus' words of encouragement:

John 16:33 ~ I have told you these things so that in me you may have peace. In this world you will have trouble. But take heart! I have overcome the world.

The Coach

In sports, most of us cannot walk up to bat and start hitting home runs with no practice at all, and we certainly can't walk onto a football field and expect to score a touchdown without training. Unless we have training and practice, we are not going to develop our abilities. That's just the way it works.

When we want to learn how to do something, and do it well, we usually need a coach. A coach is someone who encourages us, believes in us, and helps us develop our skills. A good coach wants to help us play well, and be good to our teammates and our opponents too. A coach will watch us, show us how to do things, and identify our strengths and weaknesses. A lot of time will be spent with a coach because they want us to succeed. Good coaches will help us become the best people we can be in the game and in our life.

Well, isn't that what God wants for us too? Yes it is, and God can be our coach in our daily lives, if we'll only open our hearts to Him.

Before we get to that, let's talk a little bit more about coaches. We'll use a football team as an example. On a football team, there is of course the head coach. But there are usually other coaches too, for offense, defense, and so on. Then there's the play book, containing all the different plays that the players are expected to learn. All of those things go into making a good team.

Well, if God is our coach, then the Bible is kind of like our play book. It contains God's Word, that we can read and learn from and use in our daily lives.

Much of what is contained in the Bible comes straight from Jesus—the teachings that He gave to His followers while he was here on earth. Jesus came here to teach us how to live according to God's ways. He taught us to serve God and each other, and He taught us how to pray. He healed us.

The words of Jesus are contained in the Bible, and that's great news, because it means we can still learn His ways today. Why is this so important? Because Jesus has given us many teachings to help us with our problems. We may be living in the twenty-first century, but the problems we face have stayed the same throughout human history. We all struggle in our relationships at times, we all get sick, and we all worry about things.

So the Bible is very relevant to all of our lives today. Through it, God becomes our coach, to help us become better people and to live a better life.

God did not stop there though. He has given us another way in which He coaches us, as well.

We have talked a lot so far about God and God's Son Jesus, but did you know there is a third aspect of God, called the Holy Spirit? To help understand how this can be, think of a triangle. It has three sides, but those three sides make up one triangle.

That's not a perfect description, but God is kind of like that. God is one God. But within that one God there is the Father, the Son, and the Holy Spirit. So the Father, Son and Holy Spirit make up our one true God.

I know this can be hard to understand. Theologians—people who spend their lives studying and thinking about God—have been trying to understand and explain it for hundreds of years. But the important thing to know is that although there are these three persons within God, there is still just one God, and there is no other God but Him. That's why the Bible (Deuteronomy 6:4) states, "Hear O Israel: The Lord our God, the Lord is one."

So let's learn more about these aspects of God. As we know, God sent His son Jesus here to earth to live among us. While He walked on the earth, Jesus taught people all about God. He shared meals with people, spent time with friends, shared stories with others, and healed people that doctors were unable to help. Jesus even brought dead people back to life! It was truly an amazing time. And we can read all about these events in the Bible.

As Jesus continued teaching and helping people, more and more people started to follow Him. But not everyone; there were some people who became very jealous of Jesus. So jealous, in fact, that they came up with a plan to have Him killed.

Jesus knew what these people were planning to do, but He did not try to stop it from happening. He knew that this was all part of God's plan, and that it was necessary for Him to die.

But Jesus also knew that He would not remain dead, and that in fact He would come back to life. That was part of God's plan. The reason Jesus knew all this was that He is God's Son, and God the Father, the Son and the Holy Spirit are all one.

So as the Bible tells us, "from that time on Jesus began to explain to his disciples that he must go to Jerusalem and suffer many things at the hands of the elders, chief priests and teachers of the law, and that he must be killed and on the third day be raised to life." (Matthew 16:21)

And that's exactly what happened. Jesus was killed by being nailed to a wooden cross. But on the third day after He was killed, Jesus came back to life, just as He had promised.

After Jesus came back to life, He visited His friends and shared with them some important news. He let them know that He could not stay with them much longer, and that He would be going back to be with the Father in Heaven.

Jesus' friends were very sad when they heard this. They didn't want Jesus to leave. But Jesus told them (John 16:7), "I tell you the truth: it is for your own good that I am going away. Unless I go away, the Counselor [the Holy Spirit] will not come to you, but if I go I will send him to you."

Although the disciples were sad that Jesus had to leave them, they were excited and happy when they heard this news about the Holy Spirit. And after Jesus left the earth to return to the Father, God's Holy Spirit did come to the disciples and filled them with joy and love. They then went out and began spreading the good news about Jesus, and the Holy Spirit enabled them to help, teach and heal other people too.

So you see, God loves us so much that He never wants to be apart from us, and because He loves us, God has given us His Holy Spirit. In the Bible, the Holy Spirit is also known as the Helper, the Comforter, and the Counselor. So the Spirit is like our very own coach living inside each and every one of us right now. That's why it says in the Bible (1 Corinthians 6:19), "Do you not know that your body is a temple for the Holy Spirit, who is in you, whom you have received from God? You are not your own, you were bought at a price. Therefore honor God with your body."

That passage tells us a couple of things. First, we "were bought at a price." That's referring to Jesus. He saved us from sin, and He paid with His own life.

Second, God's Spirit is inside each of us, to help us in our daily lives. How does the Spirit help us? Jesus tells us in John 14:26, "But the Counselor, the Holy Spirit, whom the Father will send in my name, will teach you all things and will remind you of everything I have said to you."

Reading this, some of us might wonder, then why is my life such a mess? If I already have the Spirit in me, why am I still struggling with blame, anger, and character issues? Well, that's a good question, but the answer is actually pretty simple. Sometimes in the craziness of life we forget to learn, listen and practice Jesus' ways.

Remember what Jesus told His friends: "The Spirit will remind you of everything I have said to you." This is why it is so important to learn about Jesus and His words to us. It's pretty hard to be reminded of something that we've never learned in the first place. But when we learn what God's ways are, the Spirit will remind us of those ways and we will be able to make much better decisions in our lives.

But what if we have problems right now, and don't know what God's ways are; is there hope? Yes, there is. God is always there and He is always with us. He will help anyone who turns to Him. If we are in this kind of situation now, the best thing we can do is let God know we want Him in our hearts and lives. God loves each of us so much that He never wants to force us into anything. He just patiently waits for us to invite Him in. Once we do that, powerful things will happen in our lives.

And the best part about this is that once we have invited and accepted God into our lives, we will get to live with Him in a fantastic relationship. Even when our body dies, we will still be able to live with God forever, because God Himself is forever, and He never wants to be apart from us.

That is so great! But how do we do all this? Again, it is through prayer. We can ask God to enter our hearts and lives, and He will. By inviting God in, we open the door for Him to start helping us live in His ways and live out the plan He has for our lives. The Bible tells us: "We are God's workmanship created in Christ Jesus to do good works which God prepared in advance for us to do." (Ephesians 2:10) God has awesome plans for each and every one of us!

If you are ready and would like to invite God into your heart and your life and start living out the awesome plan He has for you, the following prayer may help.

Prayer

Dear Jesus, thank you so much for dying for me and coming back to life for me. I believe you are God's Son. Please forgive me for all the bad things I have done. I would like to learn your ways. Please enter my heart and my life. Please fill me with Your Holy Spirit, and help me walk in Your ways. Thank you so much, Jesus.

Amen.

God is so happy that you just said that prayer. Now remember, all of your problems aren't going to magically disappear. You may still have bad emotions to deal with and you may still find yourself struggling with problems at times. But know that God is with you, and that you will never walk alone.

Having invited God into our lives, we are well on our way to becoming people with good character. It's great to know we have the wisest coach right inside of us, who will lead us and train us through life in God's way.

And yes, you will see positive changes in your life once you have accepted God into your heart. The apostle Paul talks about this in the Bible, when he writes about the "fruit of the Spirit." In his letter to the Galatians (5:22-23), Paul writes that "the fruit of the Spirit is love, joy, peace, patience, kindness, goodness, faithfulness, gentleness and self-control."

Reading those words makes me want the fruit of the Spirit in my own life. I do want more love, joy, peace, patience, kindness, goodness, faithfulness, gentleness, and self-control. I would much rather have those instead of anger, blame, judgment and hate. The fruit of the Spirit sounds so peaceful and loving. And the great news is that God is going to help us develop them all!

It's so good to realize that we can become great people with God's help. But just as an athlete doesn't become a superstar player overnight, we need training and practice to build our character. We will find ourselves in many difficult situations, and we may face many problems, but we should see those as perfect opportunities for us to practice and train in handling problems God's way. We won't do it perfectly every time, but we will succeed in the long run, because we are not on our own anymore. We have God ready to help us and coach us through anything, every day of our lives. Here's a prayer to help get started.

Prayer

Dear God, please help me handle my problems your way. Help me to see my problems as opportunities to serve you and others, so that I may do the right thing. Thank you, God.

Amen.

And let's not lose sight of Jesus' encouraging words:

John 16:33 ~ I have told you these things so that in me you may have peace. In this world you will have trouble. But take heart! I have overcome the world.

"I Quit!"

It's bad to be a quitter, right? Well, sometimes.

Quitting is not always a bad thing. Perhaps you've heard an adult say that they quit smoking or they quit doing some other things that were not good for them or their family. That kind of quitting is actually very good. When we do things that are harmful to us and our loved ones, we *should* stop doing them.

But there's another kind of quitting that's not so good, and that's having a quitting attitude. A quitting attitude is wanting to quit something, even something important and good, because you just don't feel like doing it anymore. That's the kind of quitting we are going to focus on in this chapter.

One of the best ways to develop our character is to persevere. That means to keep on working to achieve our goals, even when we feel like quitting. The Bible (Romans 5:3-4) states, "We also rejoice in our sufferings because we know that suffering produces perseverance, perseverance [produces] character, and character [produces] hope."

Now most of us would want to quit something if it's making us suffer. But what if quitting is the wrong thing to do? The Bible is clear that we should keep on doing the right thing, even if we have to suffer because of it, because that will build character, and lead us to hope. Even when it's uncomfortable or difficult, then, we should always do the right thing.

I would like to share an example from my life that taught me about perseverance, building character, and hope in God.

I have a good friend that I get together with about once a month. I'll call her Michelle. It used to be that when we would see each other, we would sometimes complain about some of the people in our lives. We would pick out things we didn't like about them and blame them for our problems. We would say things like, "Can you believe so and so said this to me? Who does she think she is?" And we would say some not so nice things about these people.

Now we knew this was not God's way, but we really didn't think too much about that; if we had, we never would have done these things. So Michelle and I continued to do this complaining and blaming people when we would get together. This did not make God very happy, because we were saying bad things about people that God created and whom He loves.

The Bible is clear that God disciplines His children when they do not follow His ways. It is also clear God does this out of love for us. The Bible tells us in Proverbs 3:11-12, "My son, do not despise the Lord's discipline and do not resent his rebuke, because the Lord disciplines those he loves, [the same way that] a father [disciplines] the son he delights in."

Well, God did indeed discipline Michelle and me, in a very real way. One night God let me know that what we were doing was very disappointing to Him.

I told Michelle about the message I had gotten from the Lord, and we reacted to it in quite different ways. I did not take the Lord's discipline very well. Michelle, on the other hand, did everything right in this situation.

Here's exactly how it happened. One night I had a dream, and in the dream God showed me all of His children going to be with Him. In this dream, Michelle and I were sitting on a bench, and I said to her, "Just wait, He's going to invite us in too." I was so excited, thinking that Michelle and I would be invited in to be with God, but nothing was happening. All of these other people were going in all around us to be with the Lord, but we were left sitting on the bench. I called out to God and said, "Hey, what about us?" He actually spoke back to me, and do you know what God said? His words were, "You have been much too critical and judgmental for my taste."

Slammed! I could not believe what I had just heard.

Now this caused great suffering to me, and I didn't handle it well. The Bible tells us to rejoice in our sufferings—I'll talk more about that in a moment—but instead of rejoicing or being thankful to God, and accepting His discipline, I did the exact opposite. I got really mad at God. Instead of apologizing for the way I had been acting, I blamed God for being mean to me. I should've been doing what the Bible tells us to do, but instead I was full of blame, judgment, and criticism. This was not good.

Then I went from being mad at God for disciplining me to being just plain sad. I felt totally rejected by God. It was awful. I should have been thankful for His message to me. I should've persevered by admitting my mistake and moving forward with God. Remember, the Bible is clear that God disciplines us out of love for us, the same way a dad disciplines his child when the child is naughty. That's basically what Michelle and I had done; we were acting up, acting badly, and God had had enough of it. He needed to discipline us.

When I told Michelle about my dream—how we had not been invited in to be with God, and His message to us—do you know what she did? She did exactly what the Bible told her to do. She thanked

God for letting her know He was not happy with her behavior. She persevered and she told God she would do whatever she needed to do to change her ways. Michelle wanted to keep moving forward with God. Michelle showed great character in that situation. Her willingness to change her ways led Michelle to have hope that God was going to teach her and help her become a better person.

I wish I could say the same for myself, but I was doing everything the opposite of what the Bible instructs. First I blamed God for being mean to me, then I felt sorry for myself, and I picked up a quitting attitude along the way. I just couldn't understand Michelle's response. She seemed so happy.

So instead of being motivated to change, and persevering the way Michelle had done, I started thinking, "I am always messing up. I can't do this. I can't seem to ever get it right. Maybe I should just quit trying." My attitude was horrible, and I felt horrible too!

Now it is important to keep in mind that God did not tell me that I was a loser, or that I was doomed to fail. God did not say, "Wow, Julie, you are such a failure, you may as well quit right now." I was thinking these thoughts on my own. All God said was that I had been too judgmental and critical to be invited in to be with Him at that moment. I was the one who started thinking all of these bad things about myself.

My outlook was all wrong, and my character went from bad to worse.

Michelle asked me why I wasn't up for the challenge to become a better person. I honestly didn't know why. I just didn't feel the way she did. Over time though, I began to understand that I was going to have to make a choice. I was miserable and not getting any better on my own, and my quitting attitude was affecting my husband and daughter. I felt so bad about myself that I began getting short-tempered with myself and others. My attitude was affecting a lot more people than just me.

Michelle knew full well she had disappointed God, just as I did. That dream hurt her just as much as it did me. But Michelle chose to allow God to help her character become better. I just wanted to be left alone in my misery. Michelle was filled with faith and hope. I, on the other hand, felt like quitting.

God then had to deal with me about my quitting attitude. He asked me why I was not thankful for His discipline.

Well, that was easy for me to answer: that dream hurt my feelings. It didn't feel good to watch God shut us out. Why should I be thankful for that?

God told me that I should be happy that He had pointed out my bad attitude.

Remember, He disciplines us because He loves us. "But why?" I asked. "Why in the world should anybody be happy when we get in trouble like this? It hurts, it doesn't feel good at all."

He taught me why I should be grateful and thankful for His discipline. I realized yes, it hurts. No, it does not feel good. And yes, it may cause suffering for a little while. But do you know what I was told? I was told that God needed to bring this to my attention now, before I got myself into even worse trouble!

I hadn't even thought about that! God was actually protecting Michelle and me by letting us know we were walking on thin ice. He rebuked us—in other words, He let us know that He did not approve of our behavior—because He knew our behavior was going to hurt us and others, and He wanted us to know this before something more serious happened.

God wasn't doing this to be mean, He was doing this to show us that He had good plans for our lives, but He could not reveal His plans to us until we were ready to handle them God's way. Here's an example that may help make this clearer.

Think of a good dad who wants to give his son an awesome gift; let's say it's a power saw.

Well, if this dad sees his son making all kinds of reckless and unwise decisions, he might hold off on giving his son that saw, because he knows if his son acted reckless with the saw, he could get hurt, or worse yet, hurt someone else.

Now this dad may try to help his son by giving him words of wisdom and advice, but ultimately it is up to the son to decide if he will take his dad's advice or just keep doing things his own way. See, the dad can't force his son to make wiser and better decisions; that is up to the son alone. The only thing the dad can do is offer advice and wait and see what his son will do.

However, if the son chooses to take his dad's advice and starts making better and wiser decisions, that's when his dad would be more likely to give his son the gift of that power saw. The dad would know then that his son would be responsible with such a powerful tool.

But even then, the dad would never just give his son the saw and say good luck. He wouldn't leave his son on his own like that. He would teach his son how to handle it safely, so that no one would get hurt. And he would help his son fully understand how to use the saw properly to make some great stuff.

Just as in the above example, God had great things in mind for both Michelle and me, but He could not move us into them until we were better able to handle our attitudes and adjust our behavior. God would not yet give us the gifts He had for us because He knew we were not ready for them. God needed to let us know that our actions were hurting us and others. He gave us advice on how to become wiser and make better decisions. For us that meant that we needed to stop criticizing and judging others. God was not going to force us to do that, but He did let us know what behaviors we needed to change, and then He waited to see how we were going respond to His advice. God had awesome gifts for both of us, but until He knew we were willing to adjust our attitudes, He was not going to give them to us.

Michelle did handle all of this God's way. She was happily moving into the plans He had for her, and she was being blessed abundantly.

I slowly came to understand that God needed me to use my words for good and to help people, instead of judging and criticizing people and tearing them down. God had good plans for my life too, but He knew I would never be able to move into them if my words were being used to hurt people. I didn't know at that time that God would someday have me writing books; all I knew was that I needed to obey and follow God by doing things His way, and that meant no more talking bad about people. I also had to stop blaming and criticizing, and I had to lose my quitting attitude.

But God didn't leave me alone in any of this. He helped me every step of the way, and He taught me how to stop blaming and start praying for people instead. God taught me how to treat others better, and He helped me understand how to stop the quitting attitude.

God never leaves us alone in our mess. Just like the good dad He is, He will always help us achieve and overcome; we just have to let Him. And we do that by asking God for help and taking the advice He gives us.

The important thing to know here is that we can either accept God's discipline and allow Him to help us, or we can choose to ignore His discipline and go our own way. God wants to move us into the wonderful plans He has for us, but we need to be willing to do things in God's way.

Proverbs 22:3 states, "a prudent man sees danger and takes refuge, but the simple keep going and suffer for it." This scripture is so true—we often do suffer when we choose to go our own way, instead of following God's way. There was not one comfortable moment I had when I tried to do things my way, but once I accepted God's discipline and allowed Him to help me, my life became much more peace-filled.

It is always our choice to make. We can either accept God's discipline, knowing He is using it to help us, or we can ignore it and wind up in worse trouble than if we would have just listened to God right from the start.

So getting back to our story, Michelle was prudent. She saw the danger in her behavior, and she asked God for help. That's what I should have done too. We need to be able to admit our wrongdoing, and we should want to change our ways when we realize they are not God's ways. And we should remember that God will always help us in this.

I am so happy I finally admitted that I was full of blame, criticism and judgment. I apologized to God for the way I had been acting towards Him and His children. I also took God's advice and started using my words for good. I was very grateful that I was able to watch how Michelle handled this, and I decided it was time for me to start doing things God's way as well.

If we have been disciplined by God, or know we are not living as God would like us to, it's important to know that He loves us, and we won't have that great feeling of peace and love in our hearts until we start doing things God's way. If we want to get our peace back and move into the awesome plans God has for us, the following prayer may help.

Prayer

Dear God, please help me listen to your rebuke. If you discipline me, I know it's for a good reason. Help me obey you and please don't let me fall into a quitting attitude. Help me to follow your ways. Thank you so much for your discipline Lord, I know it is for my good and the good of others.

Amen.

My hope in sharing all of this is that we can learn how God wants us to act, especially when we go through trials, struggles and discipline. It's also important to see where the pitfalls are and how easy it is to fall into a quitting attitude any time things start to get hard in our lives.

The important thing to know is that God wants us all to have peace and love inside. When we listen to His discipline and allow it to help us, we really do get that peace and love in our hearts. God will move us into the plans He has for us. "He (God) who began a good work in you will carry it on to completion until the day of Christ Jesus." (Philippians 1:6)

When we find ourselves in any kind of trouble and feel like giving up, this prayer may help.

Prayer

Dear God, you are my only hope and help. Please help me to follow your ways through this (say what your trouble is). Help me always do the right thing, no matter how hard it may seem. Please give me strength and help me to never quit or give up doing what is right.

Amen.

God truly has great plans for you!

Let's never forget Jesus's words of encouragement:

John 16:33 ~ I have told you these things so that in me you may have peace. In this world you will have trouble. But take heart! I have overcome the world.

The Winning Team

Do you remember in the beginning of this book how we talked about Adam and Eve? Remember how they were with God in total and perfect love until sin entered the picture?

Well, sin has not gone away. It is still in our world and it tries to lead us away from God.

There are two opposing forces on our earth today. There is good and there is evil. Sometimes we refer to them as light and darkness.

The forces of good and evil are kind of like two teams facing each other in a game. One team—the good team—is God, and following His ways will always bring us victory in our lives. That does not mean we will never have any problems; it just means when we face our problems, God will be with us. And when we handle our problems God's way, we will have peace and love inside us, and that will help everyone else around us. We all win when we stay close to God and live in His ways.

The opposing team—evil—tries to get us to make choices that do not follow God's ways. For instance, when we hear someone say that they were tempted to do something bad, that is the opposing team at work. Temptation often has something to do with sin—a violation of God's law.

We all have felt tempted and have done bad things at times. Sin is in our world, and we have all made choices we are not proud of. That's the whole reason why Jesus came to our earth in the first place. He knew we needed help and He knew we could not overcome sin without Him. That is why Jesus died for us and why He came back to life for us.

It's also why Jesus gave us teachings or lessons on how to handle our problems God's way. The Bible tells us (Peter 2:21-22), "To this you were called, because Christ suffered for you, leaving you an example, that you should follow in his steps. He committed no sin, and no deceit was found in his mouth."

The Bible also tells us in 2 Corinthians 5:21, "God made him who had no sin to be sin for us, so that in him we might become the righteousness of God."

Even though Jesus Himself was tempted by sin here on Earth, Jesus was able to say no every time, so He never did sin. He never gave into the temptation to sin. This is why we can trust Jesus. He understands what it is like to be tempted, but He also knows how to resist temptation. He never lies, and He always offers us His help and His love.

It's good for us to follow Jesus and listen to what He tells us, because He knows what's best for us at all times. And because He never did any wrong, we can be sure that His advice will always be good.

So yes, Jesus has given all of us instructions on how to handle any problem we may face, so that we can live victorious lives and avoid the traps of sin. And if we do fall into sin—and sooner or later we all do—He offers us forgiveness and help. All we have to do is turn to God.

Prayer

Dear God, please forgive me for (tell God what you have done wrong). I know I did not handle this your way. Please heal me and the people who have been hurt by this sin. Help me turn to you with all my heart so that I won't fall into this sin again.

Thank you so much Jesus for your help and forgiveness.

Amen.

Following God and His ways is the only way to avoid evil in our lives.

God knows and wants what's best for us always. He loves us, He created us, He is our Father. Anything that tries to separate us from God or that tries to stop us from following God can only hurt us. That's the opposing team and it is evil.

Following God's ways, then, is always the good and right thing to do. If anyone or anything ever comes into your life and tries to tell you otherwise, turn to Jesus. He will help you, He will protect you and He will be with you to help you face any situation. He always knows what's best for you and everyone around you.

If you are struggling with sin and know evil is near, the following prayer will help.

Prayer

Dear Jesus, please protect me. I don't want to fall into sin and temptation. Please cover me with your protection and help me to see things clearly, as they really are, so that I may continue to follow your ways. Thank you so much, God, for covering me with your love.

Amen.

"Above all, love each other deeply, because love covers over a multitude of sins." (1 Peter 4:8)

Jesus told his followers, "Pray that you will not fall into temptation." (Luke 22:40) So let's say the above prayer daily, especially if sin and temptation have been trying to keep us from God. Doing the good and right thing is very important, and God will help us do it, but we need to keep talking to Him every day and remind ourselves how much He really does love us.

You may use the prayer above, or you may want to say your own. But whichever prayer you use, it's always good to tell God exactly what you are struggling with, and to have constant reminders of just how much God truly does love you.

You should know, though, that just because we are on God's team and doing things His way does not make us perfect. Nobody is perfect, except God; that's why we all need God in our lives. We all have weaknesses and we all fall into trouble at times; that's why the Bible says, "My grace is sufficient for you, for my power is made perfect in weakness." (2 Corinthians 12:9)

This is great news. It means God does not expect us to be perfect. That takes the pressure off us—God does not love us based on how well we perform. He knows our failures, He knows we are weak, and He loves us anyway.

Not only does He love us, but God has told us that it is when we are weak that His power is made perfect. All we have to do is tell God we need Him and that we can't do it on our own. God has worked through many people in our world to do amazing things when they have surrendered to Him. When God works through our weakness, then, that's when His love and power shine the brightest, for all to see.

Let me give you an example. My husband loves baseball. It's an important part of his life and our home. We not only watch a lot of games, but also movies about baseball and baseball players.

We recently watched a program about the great New York Yankees pitcher Mariano Rivera. At one point during the show, Mariano said that his life in baseball was from the Lord. Growing up, his true passion was soccer; if he'd had a choice, he would've picked soccer over baseball in a heartbeat, but the Lord told him that he was meant to be a baseball player.

When he was starting out, Mariano had no idea God was going to make him one of the greatest baseball players ever, but that's what happened. And looking back today, Mariano knows that he never would have been able to achieve all the things he has, had it not been for God leading and guiding him. God guided him to the Yankees and made Mariano into an amazing pitcher.

But that didn't all happen right away. Mariano started out in the minor leagues, just like any other ballplayer. At first, he wasn't even planning to be a pitcher; he was a shortstop. But one day while he was playing catch, one of his coaches noticed that Mariano had a real gift for throwing the ball, and decided to try turning him into a pitcher.

Even then, though, Mariano didn't become a superstar overnight. He had to go through rigorous training, and all the while, God was helping him build his abilities and his character, so that when the time was right, Mariano would be ready for the big leagues. Mariano knew that he couldn't start right out at the top, but he accepted the training and he did it with a great attitude.

Eventually, through hard work and God's help, Mariano was ready for the major leagues, and he was called up to the Yankees. But again, he wasn't a huge success from Day One. It continued to take time, and he continued to get better, until he developed into the best relief pitcher in the game.

With that success came a huge fan base. Mariano Rivera became very popular and people love him. Even opposing players and fans of other teams like him. Why? Not just because he was good; lots of players are good, but even the good ones aren't always very popular. No, it was because Mariano treated the game with respect and because he treated people in God's way. Even when he struck out an opposing batter (and Mariano Rivera has struck out a lot of batters), he never tried to show them up or gloat. Of course he wanted to win the game, but he didn't want to make his opponents look or feel bad doing it.

Because of his success, Mariano also received financial blessings—he got paid very well by the

Yankees—yet he did not use those blessings for purely selfish gain. In fact, do you know what he has done with some of his money? After retiring from baseball following the 2013 season, Mariano has been working on a project to reach youths and many others through the construction of a church in New Rochelle, New York. He is using the lessons the Lord has taught him and the gifts God has given him to help people, so that others can share in the blessings he's received from God.

It's truly amazing to think about. Mariano is reaching so many people that might otherwise never know how much God loves them. God has been able to take something as simple as the love of sports and a man willing to obey Him to make great things happen; things that would never have been possible any other way.

Yes, God is helping many people through Mariano Rivera, but not only through Mariano. God can do amazing things through us too: things we could never do on our own, things we would never even imagine trying! God takes our weaknesses and He helps us do what would otherwise be impossible. That's why Jesus has told us that "what is impossible with men is possible with God." (Luke 18:27)

Perhaps something has happened in your life where God took a situation that seemed impossible and turned it into something that you had never even dreamed could happen. Times like that are very humbling experiences, and we realize in these moments that God really can do anything, despite all of our failures and weaknesses.

I am so grateful we have invited God into our hearts and our lives. He is so amazing. If this is all new to you, just give it time. God will shine in your heart and in your life.

Let's remember Jesus' words of encouragement:

John 16:33 ~ I have told you these things so that in me you may have peace. In this world you will have trouble. But take heart! I have overcome the world.

The Challenge

Doing things God's way can be a challenge at times. It doesn't always feel like the natural thing to do. But though it can be easy to fall into temptation, as long as we stay focused on God and remember how much He truly loves us, He will help us get through these challenging times. God knows we all sin, and He loves us anyway. So do not let your past keep you from a great relationship with God.

No matter what you have done, no matter how guilty you feel, God loves you. There is absolutely nothing you can do to make God stop loving you. He loves you unconditionally, and He has an awesome plan for your life. The Bible (Romans 8:38-39) states, "for I am convinced that neither death nor life, neither angels nor demons, neither the present nor the future, nor any powers, neither height nor depth nor anything else in all creation will be able to separate us from the love of God that is in Christ Jesus our Lord."

This chapter is dedicated to sharing a few more tools and teachings that will help us keep going strong so we can say no to sin and temptation. The things I am about to share may seem difficult but always remember that God's power is made perfect in our weakness. So don't quit; never give up.

- COURAGE -

First, let's take a look at courage. Courage doesn't usually come easily; in fact, it's pretty hard to be courageous without first facing some sort of challenge and adversity.

Courage is not so much about how we feel, as about what we do. We may be very afraid, but if we trust in God, He will give us the strength to do the right thing.

I used to think that courage meant not feeling afraid. Later I learned that courage doesn't mean that at all; it means facing and dealing with a problem, even when we *are* scared. So now I know that courage means choosing to do what we should, even if it makes us afraid.

We are all human, and having feelings is a part of being human. We are always going to have feelings, and we can't always choose what feelings to have. Sometimes they're good feelings; sometimes they're bad feelings.

But our feelings don't have to dictate how we live our lives. Firefighters must have courage to run into burning homes to rescue people. The idea of going into a burning house would scare anybody, but they don't let their fear stop them from doing good and helping others.

We also must show courage in our lives. We may not have to run into burning buildings, but there are going to be times in our lives when we feel afraid, and yet we know we must do something. Those are the times when we should trust God and rely on Him to give us the strength we need to do the right thing. When we let fear stop us from doing the right thing, that creates problems in our lives. But we don't have to let that happen.

Let's turn to God's word and take a look at what God wants us to do concerning courage. Deuteronomy 31:6 states, "Be strong and courageous. Do not be afraid or terrified, for the Lord your God goes with you; he will never leave you or forsake you."

Psalm 31:24 also states, "Be of good courage, and he shall strengthen your heart, all ye that hope in the Lord." (KJV) It is amazing what God can do through us when we turn to him for courage.

The Bible also tells us: "Ask and it will be given to you, seek and you will find, knock and the door will be opened to you. For everyone who asks receives, he who seeks finds, and to him who knocks, the door will be opened." (Matthew 7:7-8)

We may face scary situations at times, and other times we may not be sure what we should do in a certain situation. Let's not allow that feeling of uncertainty to prevent us from doing what is right. Now is the time to ask God for the courage to do the right thing. He always knows what needs to be done, so let's turn to Him, even if we are scared or unsure what to do. He will provide all the courage we need.

Prayer

Dear God, I need your strength. Please give me the courage to (tell God what you need courage for). I cannot do this without You.

Thank you, Lord.

Amen.

Please have courage, and never forget Jesus' words of encouragement:

John 16:33 ~ I have told you these things so that in me you may have peace. In this world you will have trouble. But take heart! I have overcome the world.

- PERSEVERANCE -

Another good trait that can seem challenging is perseverance. We discussed that a little bit in the chapter titled, "I Quit!" But there is still more to share on the subject of perseverance.

Hebrews 12:1 states, "Therefore, since we are surrounded by such a great cloud of witnesses, let us throw off everything that hinders, and the sin that so easily entangles, and let us run with perseverance the race marked out for us."

What does that mean? It means we should never let anything or anyone stop us from living out the plan God has for us. I love this verse because it's a great reminder that we will always face troubles that try to hinder or stop us, and that we may be easily tempted to fall into sin. We may also be distracted by our troubles, but that does not change the fact that God has a wonderful plan for us. As long as we keep our focus on Him, by reading His words in our Bible, and listening to Him, and praying about everything in our lives, He will help us to complete the task at hand.

This is such exciting news. God has given us everything we need, so that we can live out His plans for our lives. We just have to make the choice to be courageous and persevere, so that we never give up living God's way.

There's another passage from the Bible that relates to the importance of perseverance: "Consider it pure joy, my brothers, whenever you face trials of many kinds, because you know that the testing of your faith develops perseverance. Perseverance must finish its work so that you may be mature and complete, not lacking anything". (James 1:2-4)

The message, then, is, that we may achieve great things when we persevere. When we start a project, and it starts to get difficult, sometimes we're tempted to just say, "Forget it, it's too hard." But if we stick with it and keep going, eventually the job will get done. The project or task may be completely different from what we expected, but when we see it through, we may just find we have uncovered gifts, talents and blessings we didn't even know we had. You see, there is so much good that comes out of perseverance.

Perhaps you can think of times in your life when you felt like giving up, but you persevered, and later you were happy that you stuck with it. Were you amazed at how much you learned, or how much you accomplished?

This is one of the reasons why I love reading my Bible. It illustrates what we should do in our lives, by giving us direction, and a plan for how to respond to different situations. Learning from the Bible about perseverance can teach us not to give up when we're doing something important. It teaches us to keep going. God can use these experiences for our good and for the good of all the people around us too.

If there are times when you think you give up too easily, or have trouble finishing things you start, or feel like quitting the moment things start getting difficult, the following prayer may help.

Prayer

Dear God, please forgive me for giving up too easily on things. Give me the strength and courage I need to persevere. Thank you, Lord Jesus.

Amen.

Conclusion

I would like to share one more experience from my life that shows how I used to play the blame game. But through perseverance and courage I was able to overcome it with God's help and move forward in His plan for my life. The example is about this very book, *The Blame Game*. Writing this book was definitely a test of courage, perseverance, and blame for me.

When I write these books, I go to God in a special way, involving fasting and prayer. Well, at least that's what I did with the first book, entitled *Your Feelings and What God Says About Them*. During the time between writing that first book and publishing it, God gave me the title of this book, *The Blame Game*. He also told me some snippets of what was to go into this book.

But when I started writing this book, I never bothered to fast and pray to God the way I had with the first book. I just took what had been given to me and turned it into what I thought God wanted

The *Blame Game* to be. That turned out to be a huge mistake!

I rushed through the writing process, thinking, I have to get this done. As soon as I finished, I sent the book off to my publisher, thinking all along that it was what I was supposed to do. The book was published, and I gave copies to some friends who I thought would enjoy it. Thank God I only gave it to a few people.

Instead of loving the book, as I'd hoped, one of my close friends told me that she didn't like it. She said that something seemed to be missing from the book. She said, "Your first book was so great; what happened with this one?" I heard a lot of other comments that were not pleasant.

Now when I was first told that something was wrong with the book I had written, I had a choice to make. I could have gotten angry and blamed this person for being mean to me and criticizing my book; that would have been a very natural response. However, I knew it was the wrong thing to do. It's not God's way to blame and to spread anger. Plus, I knew that the person who told me this would never have said those things unless she honestly felt something was wrong with the book. So I was faced with a test: would I get angry and start blaming, and quit the project altogether, or would I go to God for help?

I did not want to fall into temptation and sin, so I took this problem to the Lord right away. I asked God to please not allow me to fall into sin, and I asked God if there was any truth in what my friend had said to me.

What came to me when I prayed about this was that I had not gone to God the way I did with the first book. I knew at this point that this had been a huge mistake.

I also knew that I had to start rewriting the whole book, but this time I had to do it the right way—God's way. And as I prayed, the Lord showed me everything else that needed to go into the book, and He also showed me that something really big had been missing from the book; HIM! That's right, I'd written this entire book and left out God Himself. Yikes! This was really not good!

I knew serious changes needed to be made. I was very upset and scared because I had already sent the book to my publisher, who had already printed many copies of the book. Well, no matter how upset I felt, I knew I needed to redo the entire book. But, this in a way, this was a great test of my courage. It meant I needed to tell my friends and publisher, "Sorry, but the book I gave you is not the book God wanted me to write."

That's a hard thing to do: admitting to everyone that you've made a big mistake. I was afraid of being rejected, and I felt embarrassed. I needed courage to get through this, but I knew it was the right thing to do. I also knew that despite my failures and weaknesses, I could trust God to fix everything. I just had to be courageous and take that step.

I asked God for help, and sure enough, He gave me the strength I needed. I made phone calls, and I sent e-mails. I told people to just throw that book away. I told them I had rushed through the writing process, and hadn't gone to God the way I should have.

Once I made the decision to do the right thing, God helped me to persevere. I knew I could have easily fallen into the temptation to just quit and say forget it, but I knew from my past experiences with quitting that this was not the right thing to do. Instead, I went to Jesus right away, and He helped me rewrite this entire book. He did not condemn me, nor did He make me feel like a failure. Rather, I felt loved, and He was able to use all of these experiences to help me rewrite *The Blame Game.*

That's not to say it was easy; rewriting the whole book was a difficult thing to do. It took a lot of time and patience, but God gave me the strength to move forward with Him. And this time He made the book the way He wanted it to be.

This experience has taught me some very valuable lessons about blame, courage and perseverance, and now I know what I have to do next time God gives me an idea for a book. I learned a lot through this experience, and I'm thankful for that now. At the time I didn't feel happy about any of this, but because God led me through this His way, I can now look back and realize that this book has truly been a blessing to me. My sincerest prayer is that it will be a blessing to you too.

The reason I wanted to share this experience with you is that we all make mistakes. We all fall into sin at some point in our lives, and we can all be tempted at times to blame others when things go wrong. There will also be times when people say things that really hurt us but that's OK. Instead of getting angry and blaming others, let's just take it to the Lord. That is the best way to keep peace in our hearts.

All we have to do is tell God what is troubling us. It's nothing to be afraid of.

If there is something we need to change, let's be courageous, and do the right thing. If we stick with God, He will always help us to persevere and deal with anything, even our worst mistakes and failures. God is able to help us overcome any problem we will ever face, including the blame game!

Prayer

Dear God, please help me stop playing the blame game. Thank you so much for your words in the Bible. Please help me to live by them every day of my life, so that I can have peace and live out the awesome plan you have for me.

Amen.

Never forget Jesus' words of encouragement:

John 16:33 ~ I have told you these things so that in me you may have peace. In this world you will have trouble. But take heart! I have overcome the world.

Suggested Reading List

The Holy Bible

Joyce Meyer, Battlefield of the Mind for Kids

Joyce Meyer, Battlefield of the Mind for Teens

Joyce Meyer, Battlefield of the Mind

Other Books by Julie Chapus:

Your Feelings and What God Says about Them

Note from the Author

If you have found this book helpful, please leave me a comment at:

www.christforkidsministries.com

I'd love to hear from you.

Julie

www.ingramcontent.com/pod-product-compliance
Lightning Source LLC
Chambersburg PA
CBHW061957070426
42450CB00011BA/3124